How Eagle Got His Good Eyes

Published by Willowisp Press
801 94th Avenue North, St. Petersburg, Florida 33702

Printed in the United States of America

2 4 6 8 10 9 7 5 3 1

ISBN 0-87406-743-X

HOW EAGLE GOT HIS GOOD EYES

Written and illustrated by the Grade 5 and Grade 7 students of Oscar Blackburn School, South Indian Lake, Manitoba, Canada:

Earl Anderson, Jared Anderson, Lambert Anderson, Curtis Dysart, Dorothy Dysart, Beatrice Linklater, Owen Linklater, Rosalyn McLeod, Barry Moose, Bert Soulier, Sidney Soulier, Andy Spence, Stewart Spence, Vanessa Tait, Jennifer Wood

Coordinated by teachers Jerome Greencorn and Launa Ruttle

Cree translation by Margaret Moose, with assistance from Shirley Ducharme

ABOUT THE CREE INDIANS

For centuries, the Cree Indians were
forest-dwelling people of Canada.
They were excellent hunters, trappers,
and fishers. Their homes were tepees
covered with hides or birchbark.

Some bands later moved to grassy
areas. They were called the Plains
Cree and became known as
buffalo hunters.

Although most Cree still live
in Canada, some now share
reservations with other Indian
tribes in the United States.

We dedicate this legend to our families,

especially our elders, for giving us

legends of animals in Northern Manitoba.

Their traditional way of storytelling has

inspired us to write this legend.

—*The Authors and Illustrators*

A long, long time ago in northern Canada, there lived Eagle. Eagle had no eyes. He always bumped into trees and crashed into bushes.

He could catch some animals because he could hear and smell well. But Eagle didn't catch much food because he couldn't see.

ᑳᔨᐣ, ᑳᔨᐣ ᐊᑌ ᑫᐌᐣ_ᐅˣ
ᐊᐣᑫˣ, ᑫ ᐊᔾᐤ ᒥᑭᔪᐤ. ᓇᐊ·ᐧ
ᑭ ᐅᑭ ᐅᐣᑫᕒᑦ. ᑳᐴ ᑭᐸᐊᐧᐣᑦᕒᐤ
ᕒᐦᑕ ᐊᑭ· ᓂᐊ ᐁ ᐸᐧᑲᑭ ᕒᕒˣ
ᐅᐱᔪᔨ. ᑫ ᑳᐣᑭᑕᐤ ᐨ ᑳᕒᐣᐊᐧ
ᐊᐣᐦᐧ ᐯᕒᐣ ᑭᐊ· ᐁᑭ ᐊᐦᐁᐨ ᐊᑭ·
ᐁᑭ ᐊᐦᐊᐸᐧᐣᐧ. ᒪᑳ ᓇᐊ·ᐧ ᒥᑭᔪᐤ
ᑭ ᐅᑭ ᐅᐨᐦᐃᒥᐊᐦᐅᐤ ᐊᐊ·ᕒᑐ
ᐁᑳᐩ ᐁᑭ ᐅᑭ ᐊ·ᐱᐧ.

A man lived near Eagle. His name was Nanabush. Nanabush was a trickster. He would trick any animal if he had the chance.

ᐊᐍᐤ ᐊᐊᐎᓂᑊ ᐃᕆᓂ ᑲᑌᐧ ᑭᕆᐊᐧ
ᑭᐞᐁᑕ ᔕᑐᐤ ᒥᑭᕛᐊᐧ
ᑭᓂ ᑕᐊᐧᐁᐧ ᔕ ᑌᕆᖁᐤ ᐱᑯ ᑕ ᓂᑊᐃ
ᐱ ᕈ ᑭᐊᐧ ᑭᓱᓂ ᐱᔪ ᐃᓂ ᐸᑕ ᑊᐃᑯᕆ.

Nanabush wanted to be chief of all his people.
He thought that he needed a headdress.

"With a headdress, I could become chief,"
he thought.

ᓇ ᓇ ᐳᓂᐦ ᑭ ᓄᐦᑌ ᐅᑭᒫᑲᓂᐅᐧᐅ
"ᐅᑭᒫᑲᓂ ᐊᓂᑐᓂᐸ ᐊᔮᔭᓂ, ᓂ ᑲᑭ
ᐅᑭᒫᑲᓂᐅᐧᐸ," ᑭ ᑌᓭᑕᒡ.

He knew that Eagle had the biggest and the best feathers. Nanabush decided to shoot Eagle to get the feathers.

Nanabush tried and tried to shoot Eagle. But he couldn't shoot the bird because Eagle was flying too fast and too high.

Nanabush had to get a new idea.

ᑫ ᑭᐢᑭᓂ̄ᐁᑕᑦ ᒥᑭᓯᐘ ᐁᐊᓴᓂ̄ᐟ
ᒥᐢᑌ ᒣᑳᓇ ᐊᑳ ᒣᓇ
ᐁᒣᐟᐦᐘᓯᐟᑐᓂ̄ ᑭᕽ. ᓇᓇᐳᐢᐦ
ᑭ ᐁᑌᓂ̄ ᑕᑦ ᑕᐸᐢᑭᐢᐘᐟ ᒥᑭᓯᐘ
ᓇᓇᐸᐢᐦ ᑭᑯᒥᑕᐤ ᑕᐸᐢᑭᐘ'
ᒥᑭᓯᐘ ᒹᑲᑦᐘ- ᑭ ᐅᒋ
ᑲᐢᑭᑕᐤᑕᑕᐘᐦᐅᐟ ᐅᐦᐅᐱᓂ̄ ᓯᐟᓴ.
ᐅᓴᑦ ᒣᑭᓴᐤ ᐁ ᑭᓴᓇ̄ᐟ ᐊᑳ
ᒣᓇ ᐃᐱᒣᐦᐠ ᐁ'ᒣᓂ̄ᐟ.
ᓴᐤ ᑕᓂᓯᐟᑫᑭᑐᑕᐘᐠ ᑭᐁᑎᓂ̄ᑕᑦ
ᓇᓇᐳᐢᐦ.

Nanabush put a net between two trees.
He tied jackfish and pickerel to the net.
Then, he hung a giant sturgeon from one of
the trees. Eagle would smell that for sure.

Not far away, Eagle was very hungry.
He was really surprised and excited when
he smelled the fish.

ᑕ ᐸᕆᐧ ᑫᒥᐱ-
ᒥ ᑭᕈᐤ ᒍ ᓓ ᐊᐊᐧᕒ�???? ᐊᐧ???
ᐊᐦ ???? ????ᐅᐦ�`????. ???ᑕᑕᗑᐧᕒᐦ
???ᑐᐸᓓᐧ Lᐊ Ꮐᕒᐧᐦᐁᐧ ???ᑕᪿ
ᐁᐸ ᕒᐧ ᑭᓓᔦᐊᐧ

Eagle followed the smell.
He crashed into many trees
but he did reach the fish . . .
and the net.

Eagle was very angry and
he waved his claws.

Nanabush was afraid to
go near Eagle. He had no
more arrows, so he decided
to make a deal with the bird.

Γᑭᐞᣳ ᖬᓇᓇᐧᑊᐧ<ᒀᣳ. Γᒡᐟ
ᒥᐣᑕᑭᐧ ᑭᐊᑎ ᓇᑊᒷᐣᑯᒉᣳ
ᒪᑭ ᐅᒥᒼᣳ ᑭ ᐅᑎᑌᣳ ᐊᓂᐦᐃ ᑮᓇᐧᑕᐧ
ᐊᑭᐧ ᐊᐋᐸᕊ.
Γᑭᐞᣳ ᑭᐧᐢᐣᣳ ᑭᑭᒉᐊᐧᒉᣳ
ᒪᐅᓂ ᐁᑕᐧᑕᐣᑕᐦᐁᐱᓇᐧᐧ ᐊᐣᑲᕊᐦ
ᐊᐟᑯᓂᑌᣳ ᑭᒉᐊᐧᐣ ᑕᓇᐧᣳᐧ
Γᑭᒉᐊᐧ. <ᒀᣳᣳ ᐊᐊᐧᕈᑕ ᐊᑲᐣᑭᐧ
ᑭ ᐅᒥ ᐊᑊᐁᐧᣳᣳ. ᑭᓂ ᑭᐁᑎ ᓇᑕᣳ
<ᑐᐣᑭᑊᣳᑕᑕᓇᣳ ᐅᐦᐅ ᐱᓇᐧᕊᐦ.

Nanabush said, "I want some feathers. What do you want?"

Eagle replied, "I'll give you some feathers if you give me your eyeballs."

Eagle made Nanabush swear to the Great Spirit, Manitou.

Nanabush crossed his fingers and swore, "I will give Eagle my eyes if he gives me some feathers."

ᓇᓇᐳᓐ" ᑭᐃᐅᐧ ᒥᑭᔭᐸᐧ·,"ᓕᐸᐧᓇ
ᓂᐳᑕᐁᐧ·ᅙᡃᐧᐸᐧᐢ ᖃᐸᐧᐳ ᖃ ᐁ
ᐸᐳᑕᐁᐧ· ᅙᑕᒪᐳ?"
ᐸᓕᅙᐣᐳ ᓂᓕᐸᐧᓇ ᓕᅙᓂᐯᓐᖃᕒᐸᐧ·
ᐃᐅᐧ ᒥᑭᔭᐤ.
ᒥᑭᔭᐤ ᑭᕒᑯᒥ"ᐁᐧᐧ ᑕᓐᐱᐨᐧᐧᐧ·
ᑭᖪᐧᐳᐅᐧ·.
ᓇᓇᐳᓐ" ᑭᐁᒪ"ᐅᐧ·ᓇᐨ ᐅᕒᖪᓕ
ᐊᐸᐧ· ᑭ ᓇᐧᑯᐅᐧᐧ, "ᓂᐸ ᓕᅙ
ᒥᑭᔭᐤ ᓂᐧᖃᕒᐸᐧ· ᖃᐧᐱᐳ ᓕᅙᒥ
ᐊᓐ"ᐧ ᐅᓕᐸᐧ ᓇ.

Nanabush broke the promise. He took fish eyes from the dead sturgeon and put them in Eagle's sockets.

"Where is my eyesight?" Eagle squawked.

Nanabush said, "It's nighttime. You can't see in the dark."

Eagle nodded. "Take ten feathers from my body."

Nanabush plucked fifteen feathers and ran away.

ᓇᓇᐳᐢᐦ ᑫᐯᑯᓇᐨ ᑲᑭ ᐃᓯᓇᐢᑯᒧᐟ
ᑎᓴᑳᐧ- ᓇᒣᐤ ᐅᐢᑭᓯᑳᐧ ᑭ ᒥᓃᐤ·
ᒥᑭᓯᐘ
"ᑫᑳᐧᑐ ᐁᑲ ᑯ ᐅᒋ ᐘᐱᓴᑐ", ᐁᑌᐧᐦᐃᑕᐤᒥᑭᓯᐤ.
"ᐊ+ ᑎᐱᐢᑳᐤ ᐅᒪ·ᒧᓈ ᑲᑭ ᐚᐱᑐ
ᐁᑎᐱᐢᑲᕽ:" ᐃᑌᐤ ᓇᓇᐳᐢᐦ.
ᒥᑭᓯᐤ ᓇᓇᒥᐢᑫᐧ ᓃᐤ "ᐅᑎᓇ ᒥᑕᐦᐟ
ᓂᒣᑳᐧᓇ ᓂᓴᐃᐧᕽ ᐅᒋ:"
ᒥᑕᓂᓴᓴᐠ ᒣᑳᐧᓇ ᑲᒪᓂᐱᑕᐠ
ᓇᓇᐳᐢᐦ ᐊᑳᐧ ᑲᑕᐸᓯᐦᐟ.

Manitou, the Great Spirit, was watching from the sky. He knew Nanabush broke a vow to him. Manitou was very angry. Using lightning, Manitou gave Eagle really good eyesight. Then he burnt away the net that was covering the bird.

Eagle spread his wings and thanked Manitou. Eagle flew away.

ᑭᒋ ᒪᓂᑐ ᑭ ᐅᑎ ᑲᓇᐋᐧᐱᓊ ᐃᐣᐱᒥˣ.
ᑭ ᑭᐣᑭᔕᑕᐨ ᐁᐱᑯᓇ ᒣᐤᐧ ᑲᑭ ᐃᐱᐧ
ᐊᑐᒐᒪᑯ "ᐧᔆ.
ᑲᐧᔭᐣ ᑭᑭᔕᐊᐧᔪᐤ. ᐱᐢᔪᐤ ᐃᐣᑯᐤᐅ
ᐁᔭᐸᒋᒐᔎᔮᐣ ᒪᓂᑐ, ᑭᑦᐢᐤ
ᒥᑭᔕᐊᐧ ᑲᐧᔭᐣ ᐊᐧᐱᐊᐧᐤ. ᑲᓂ
ᑭᐊᐣᐸᔪᔪᐤ ᐊᓂ"ᐃᐊ ᐊᐧᔭ
ᑲᐸᓇᑲᒃᔆ ᐊᐊᐧ ᐱᐢᔭ ᔮᐣ.
ᒥᑭᔪᐤ ᑭᑕᔮᐊᐨ ᐅᑕᑕᑲᓇ "ᐊᑲᐧ
ᑭᓇᓂᐟ ᐣᑯᔪᐤ ᑭᒋ ᒪᓂᑐᐊᐧ.
ᒥᑭᔪᐤ ᑭᐊᑎ ᔭᐯᐧᓇᐤ.

He still didn't fly properly because fifteen feathers were missing.

He saw Nanabush running. Eagle glided down and snatched his feathers from Nanabush's quiver.

Then, he picked up Nanabush and dropped him in a river.

Nanabush had to swim to shore. He was wet and cold.

ᒪᐊᐧ ᐸᐧ ᔕᓐᐦ ᕽᑊᐱ ᑭ ᐅ ᒋ
ᑭᐱᒥᓇ ᐅᔕ ᒥᒐᒐᐦᐧᓂᕽᐅᕽᐦ
ᐅᒋᐸᐧ ᐊ ᐊᐱᓇ ᒪᐦᐸᕽᐅᐅ ᑭᐦ.
ᑭᐊᐧᐸᑐ ᐊ ᐊᐊᐳᐣᐦᐊ ᐊᐱᐸᑕ ᓂ.
ᒥᑭᔕ ᑭ ᐋᔕᐸᓂᐦᐳ ᐊᐸ
ᑭᒪ ᐸᐦᐁ ᐅᑊᐸᐧ ᐊ ᐊ ᐊᐳᐣ
ᐅᐸᐊᐧᒐ ᐸᐧ ᓂᐊᐧᐱ ᐅᒋ.
ᐊᐸ ᐸᑭ ᐅᐱ ᐊᓇ ᐊ ᐊ ᐳᐣᐦᐊ
ᐊᐸ ᑭ ᑊᐱ ᐱ ᐊ ᔕᐯ.
ᐸ ᒐᐸᑊᐦᐊᐸ ᐊ ᐊ ᐳᐣ ᐊ ᔕ
ᐊᔕᐳᐯ ᐊᐸ ᐊ ᑭ ᐸᐊᐧ ᒋ.

He also lost his quiver and all his food in the water.

Eagle felt sorry for Nanabush. With his good eyesight, Eagle spotted a big fish.

He grabbed it and brought it to Nanabush.

They shared the fish and Nanabush apologized.

They were friends the rest of the season . . .

ᑭᐗᓂᑕᐤ ᐅ'ᑦᐗᑕᑳᓂᐗᐟ ᐊᓯᒋ
ᒥᓯᐍ ᐅᒣᒋᑦ ᓂᐯᕽ.
ᒥᑭᓭᐤ ᑭᑭᑎᒪᑭᓇ ᐍᐤ ᓇᓇᐳᐡᐦᐊ
ᐃᓃᑯᐦ ᑲᓇᐦᐊᐱᐟ, ᒥᑭᓭᐤ ᐘᐸᒣᐤ
ᒥᐡᑕ ᓈᓭᐘ.
ᑭ ᐅᑎᑎᓃᐤᐊᑳᐧ ᐱᒣᓃᐤ ᓇᓇᐳᐡᐦᐊ
ᑭᐊ ᑳᐦᒪᑐᐘᐠ ᐊᓂᐦᐃ ᑭᓈᓭᐘ ᐊᑳᐧ
ᓇᓇᐳᐡᐦ ᐳᓂᓃᑕᒍᐎᑉ ᑳᑴ ᒋᒣᐤ
ᒥᑭᓭᐘ.
ᑭᐍᒋᐘᑳᓂᒥᑐᐘᐠ ᑳᐯᓃᐱᐣ.

. . . until Nanabush tried to trick Eagle again.

ᐸᐱᒪ ᐴ ᐊ ᐊᐣ ᐳ ᐣ" ᐁ ᐧ ᕝ ᐁ ᐧ
ᒋ ᔑ" ᐊ ᕊ ᒥ ᐱ ᔕ ᐊ ᐧ

Kids Are Authors™
COMPETITION
Books written by children for children

....

School Book Fairs, Inc., established the Kids Are Authors™ Competition in 1986 to encourage children to read and to become involved in the creative process of writing. Since then, thousands of children have written and illustrated picture books as participants in the Kids Are Authors™ Competition. The winning books in the annual competition are published by Willowisp Press® and distributed in the United States and Canada.

For the official rules on the Kids Are Authors™ Competition, write to:

In the U.S.A.,

Trumpet Book Fairs
Kids Are Authors™ Competition
801 94th Avenue North
St. Petersburg, Florida 33702

In Canada,

Trumpet Book Fairs
Kids Are Authors™ Competition
257 Finchdene Square, Unit 7
Scarborough, Ontario M1X 1B9

Published winners in the annual Kids Are Authors™ Competition

1994: **Where's Our Teacher?** (U.S. winner)
by fourth graders of Rio Bravo-Greeley Elementary School, Bakersfield, California.
How Eagle Got His Good Eyes (Canadian winner)
by fifth and seventh graders of Oscar Blackburn School, South Indian Lake, Manitoba.
Lunch with Alex (Honor Book)
by first graders of Hollis Hand Elementary School, LaGrange, Georgia.

1993: **A Day in the Desert** (U.S. winner)
by first graders of Robert Taylor Elementary School, Henderson, Nevada.
The Shoe Monster (Canadian winner)
by first and second graders of North Shuswap Elementary School, Celista, British Columbia.

1992: **How the Sun Was Born** (U.S. winner)
by third graders of Drexel Elementary School, Tucson, Arizona.
The Stars' Trip to Earth (Canadian winner)
by eighth graders of Ecole Viscount Alexander, Winnipeg, Manitoba.

1991: **My Principal Lives <u>Next</u> <u>Door</u>!**
by third graders of Sanibel Elementary School, Sanibel, Florida.
I Need a Hug! (Honor Book)
by first graders of Clara Barton Elementary School, Bordentown, New Jersey.

1990: **There's a Cricket in the Library**
by fifth graders of McKee Elementary School, Oakdale, Pennsylvania.

1989: **The Farmer's Huge Carrot**
by kindergartners of Henry O. Tanner Kindergarten School, West Columbia, Texas.

1988: **Friendship for Three**
by fourth graders of Samuel S. Nixon Elementary School, Carnegie, Pennsylvania.

1987: **A Caterpillar's Wish**
by first graders of Alexander R. Shepherd School, Washington, D.C.

1986: **Looking for a Rainbow**
by kindergartners of Paul Mort Elementary School, Tampa, Florida.

To order Kids Are Authors™ titles, call Willowisp Press® at **1-800-877-8090**.
In Canada, call **1-800-387-5360**.